Petals and Embers

Poems by and for the Ruminating Mind

Teertha Anil

Leadstart
INKSTATE

ISBN 978-93-5438-861-3

First published in India 2021 by Leadstart Inkstate
A Division of One Point Six Technologies Pvt Ltd

119-123, 1st Floor, Building J2, B - Wing,
Wadala Truck Terminal, Wadala East,
Mumbai 400022, Maharashtra, INDIA
Phone: +91 96999 33000
Email: info@leadstartcorp.com
www.leadstartcorp.com

Disclaimer: The views expressed in this book are those of the Author and do not pertain to be held by the Publisher.

Editor: Sanjhee Gianchandani
Cover: R. Maharaja
Illustrations: Kodhai B Narayanan
Layouts: Kshitij Dhawale

To all the women, men and anyone in between or beyond,

who are carrying an entire, vulnerable universe within themselves.

About the Author

The author is an ambitious, out of place, chronic daydreamer. Her name is Teertha and she is 22 years old. She is from God's Own Country – Kerala but at times feels particularly godless. She has struggled with her mental health for almost five years now, though it has in no way affected her passion for life. She prefers to be called 'distinct', not 'different'. She has very recently developed a love for English classical literature and Milky Bar. She has dabbled with love, the ceremony of getting a college degree, and of course with being society's idea of perfection and has failed miserably in all of them. Now, she is grappling with living and in doing that happily. And so far, so good.

Acknowledgements

Sumit Sir was the backbone of the entire venture long before the idea of the book ever entered my mind. I showed him my first poem and he took time out of his busy life to explain the good, the bad, and the average with so much patience and seriousness, that I started taking my writing seriously and not just as the scribblings of a silly girl. He, with his inherent kindliness and crystal-clear comprehension, was my mentor throughout. I couldn't be more grateful or blessed to have a teacher like him.

I also wish to thank my dear, dear family who believed in me unconditionally and were my cheerleaders and best friends throughout. Thank you, Amma, Papa and Chocho.

I wish to thank my dear Naureen ma'am who was like my fairy godmother, who was a balm for my injuries with her benevolent words and sensible advice.

I would like to thank Zaha, who was the biased editor who would make me feel confident about my work with the disproportionate amount of praises she would lavish on my poems before I got an unbiased review from Sumit sir.

I would like to thank Ratnesh ma'am who stood by me like a wise, elderly sister through thick and thin and made me see the beauty in life and not just the moroseness.

I would also like to thank Dr Preeti Jacob for lifting me from my deep burrow of gloom and bringing me back to life.

I would like to thank Jo for being more motherlike than most mothers and keeping me grounded with her calming presence.

And how can I not thank Kodhai, who is the artist responsible for the beautiful illustrations that adorn this book?

Finally, I would like to thank my angel, my Ammooma or Ammu for being the coolest grandma on earth.

I would also like to thank anyone and everyone who helped me grow as a person. Thank you.

Contents

Poems

THE ROBE OF GOLD

Don't let me get swept away in this tide that leaves no traces.
Chain me if you must, to the burden that is my privilege to bear;
chain me with the dreams, hopes, and aspirations of a whole
generation -
A generation that suffered and saved and then died,
that is my inheritance.

Chain me with my legacy that is rooted in the soil,
in the sweat and toil of a young ragged boy
who dared to dream,
dared to dream of a life that didn't depend
on the whims of the fickle earth for a day's sustenance.

Mark me with the blood he spilled as he faced bullets,
with his unshed tears as he smiled and saluted
facile, entitled, potbellied seniors,
entitled by birth, entitled by fate.

Mark me and let it be my reminder,
as the soul of the emaciated boy; let the man nod and stand in
attention
as the gluttons took credit for his work,
with nothing but the power of a few extra stars on their shoulders,
the only path that led to light for him.

He wove a cloth of gold, gold bought at a huge price as he walked
down that road.
He wrapped his little girl in that cloth of gold
and bid her take care.

Wrapped in that gold, the little girl poured her all into her lessons to
preserve that gold
she is a woman now and she has forgotten that she bears the robe of
gold;
she was chosen to wear it,
chosen to fulfil the dreams of a generation,
the dreams of a young ragged boy.

She has forgotten the robe,
she has forgotten the burden which her privilege is to bear.
She is the hope of the little boy.
His last standing chance.
I am the last standing chance.
Remind me of the robe of gold, chain me to my purpose,
for his sake, for my sake.

A Prayer ✑

Let me free misery,
Do thou the mighty pity me.
Fly far away and leave me in the heaven of purgatory;
If not the one of bliss
or let me fly far from thee who flies not from me.
Set me uninjured in the world of happiness
set your sway on that which injures
leave me, a simpleton to trip over her own feet.

Prey not on the meek,
we already cower in the shadows of the fierce.
Don't trample over the weed,
fight thou he who is thy equal.
Don't trample over the meek,
let me die only once at once,
not every day for the rest of the days.

ANOTHER PRAYER ✣

Come bless my sullen way!
Do thou felicity, bind me with your hallowed sway.
From thee who escapeth the best escapists of woe,
let me not escape.

Find me with a store of entwined dreams;
Find me entwined with the twine
of that tree that heals
those thy twin maimed.

Free me from this sickly teal,
I aspire towards the earthy browns
reserved for those hardy deep down.

Give me hardships a hundred, nay, a thousand
But shadow my days,
Let thy rays
guide me away from the bane
of thy brother's strain.
Enfold me in thy fane,
nay encompass me in thy sweet refrain.

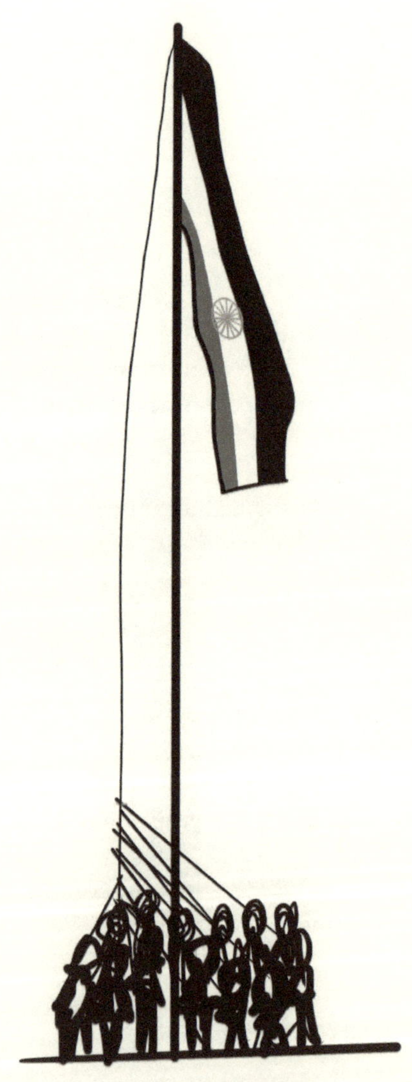

THE NATION

It is an everyday plebiscite,
the tricolour a barely surviving idea.
is the saffron in the valley,
the same shade as the one worn by those who preach love?
Is it the same as the one worn by those who preach hatred?

Is it a western modality
or just a desperate attempt at unity?
Who's to say what am I and what's mine?
Who are they to say the red in their blood is green?

Who's to say that colours mean anything?
The conflict is our own,
birthed by us, nurtured by us, defended by us.

Why is the rainbow burdened with the shame?
When the darkness lies in our minds.
Why are the Gods to blame
when the unholiness lies in our hearts?

IN THE FROW

Fairy lights, the good times,
All a hopeless mirage.
The world's crashing down,
all the ice is melting now.
But the stubbornness of us
will remain in the frow.

Higher walls, higher heels,
higher skyscrapers, louder screams.
all left unheard
by the cherries on the top.

The world's crashing down,
let's sing as it sinks,
all the ice is melting now.
but the stubbornness of us
will remain in the frow.

THE VULNERABILITY OF OUR UNIVERSE 

Fighting a battle inside out,
internal bleeding, not just collateral damage.
The wide expanse which we carry within us;
hanging by the veins of an uncut hand.

Our smile just a forged reflection of theirs,
our lives reliant on a fine balance
of fate or a slight swerving in that unending universe
that guides us from the tips to our toes,
our lips and our woes.

The entire universe conspires to help them.
Who will help us?
When our universe is collapsing in on itself.

THE LOVE POTION

Drunk on that potent potion,
two drops too many would kill.
We will drink with care, we agreed,
A childish agreement by two children
who naught knew
that the drink gives a choice
only so long as it isn't greeted by your lips.

They drank and then they stopped.
They had sealed their fates.
Stopping mattered not;
they were now mates.
The potion mated with their blood,
ran a race in their veins,
webbed in their heart,
now it is too late.

They are enchanted by the sweet melody
that sings in their breasts.
They can't undo the webbing
without cutting open
what's left of their will.
They are drunk on the potion;
it is now the king of hearts
who reigns over the rest of their days.

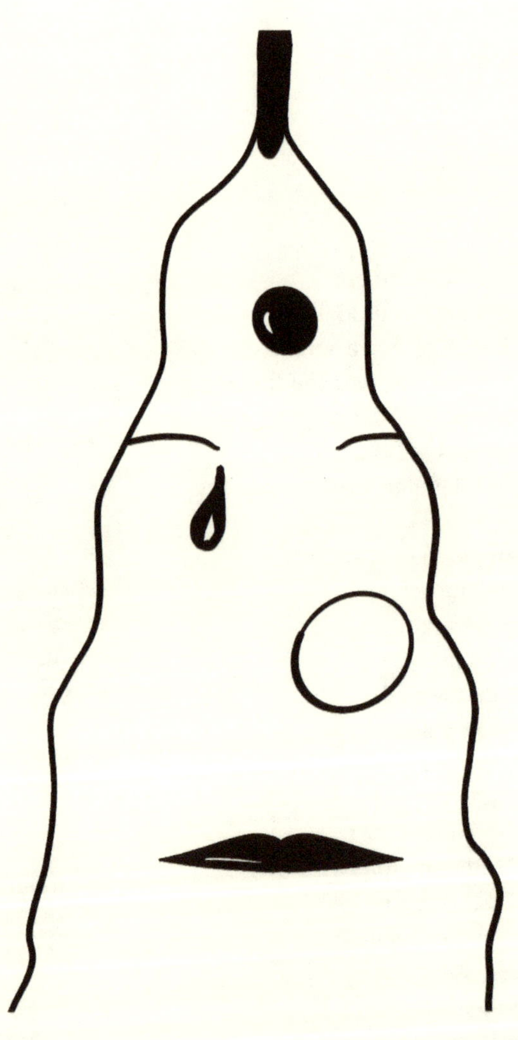

THE RED

Trickles down;
It doesn't fizzle out.
The red pollutes you;
you pollute the world.
Lakshmi to abomination;
The gods no longer want you;
your mother no longer wants you.

But of course, pray
when the red doesn't want you.
Fie on the people
who hate you for your skin.
Why not fie on the people
who hate you for your blood?
Who don't touch you
as if your long raven hair
was washed in red,
like Draupadi of yore.

I say, paint the world red.
Paint your hair red.
Paint the sacred red.
With your presence,
in all your unholiness,
paint man's decree red.

Don't be apologetic
for not being a man.
Be apologetic
for not being a woman.
Lakshmi you are upon birth;
Lakshmi you remain once a month,
when you face your own sweet holy blood.

THE PERPETUAL DUSK

Blinking through the foliage;
The sun is setting over a day;
The sky fades to a grey.
The peeping pinks and oranges;
Small bursts of a hope
that never stays.

Small streaks of yellow just a lucky coincidence,
nothing of incidence.
Always just leaking,
always just peaking;
the globe of orange
dreams of greeting the day.

The horizon just a few yards away;
The vast ocean above;
The clouds all around
all a dream, it will stay.
In perpetual dusk;
the essence lost, just a husk,
the mind remains.

DREAMLAND

Irreverent reveries, one too many.
Dreamy abstractions, far too many.
Round and round it goes,
Down the rabbit hole, she goes.
She is falling and falling
into this bottomless pit;
an enticing ditch.
Footholds, there are none.
Protruding branches, just cinematic fun.

Round and round it goes
down the rabbit hole, she goes
into this chasm of sad, sad joy.
It is cataclysmic.
This failure on sanity's part.
The bursts of gaiety,
in all her naivety,
She mistakes it for a departure to hope.
Departure it is, from hope.

Round and round it goes,
down the rabbit hole, she goes.
It is a trench of unfulfilled dreams,
a ditch full of corpses of screams.
No light, no prayers, nor cries for help

Travel through these godless paths.
No strings of silk, nor wool
reach its wool gathering doe.
She has now become earth's foe.

Now she is far gone,
she has bid adieu to the ground
for far too long.
Adieu! Adieu! sweet land,
I shall drink from this bitter stream,
disguised as a sweet dream.

VADAMALLI

The summer zephyr
stirs the Vadamalli.
Beautiful in its strength,
beautiful in its small-boned glory.
Wrapped in its purple hues,
it stands proud and straight
in poverty, drought, and rain.

A template, for the ideal woman,
a template, for the ideal human.
Flourishes in the menacing heat,
adorns the night, overcomes defeat.

Droop, it does not,
bend, it will not.
It's fluorescence, a jewel for the night.
for all its might,
it does die, a magnificent death.
A skeleton of a perennial warrior,
the bones of a proud female,
it's dignity, it's holy grail.
Erect, dry, only of life,
looking upon, only the sky.

A SAFE SPACE

Find me a safe space,
for all the roses,
for all the thorns,
for all the ghastly gashes.
Find me a place,
where our God reserves judgement.
Adharma only upon hurting,
that which is not ours to hurt.
Dharma only upon helping,
that which is not ours to help.

Find me a place
for my past and present vices,
for my now lifeless choices,
for all my untouched horizons,
for all my unmet visions.

Give me three more, only three more
measures of land.
One for each of the folded hands;
each of the unheard demands,
To rest my head on,
heavy from three generations
worth of hopes
and dreams slowly etched with care

on to the planks of my crib.

Find me a place
where my screams for help
don't just echo back to me.
Find me a place
where they are embraced,
hushed and caressed
with gentle care
by the objective breeze.

Find me a place
that can contain my herculean will
with a ceiling
tall enough for my head, unbowed still,
for my land of brimming passions
on which the sun doesn't set.
Where rivers of sweat
carry my essence
to the vast sea
of my efforts sweet.

Find me a place,
where there is order
in this blank verse.
Find me a place,
that can contain the wind.
Find me a place,
where I can write my victory hymn.

BEHOLDEN

Beholden I am to these magic carpets,
These potent vessels of wisdom
that carry me off to what lies beyond
the edges of my mind's vision.
The warm embrace of that woody scent,
like the gay calls of my trusty friends
lure me away from all that is cruel;
All that is wicked.

Beholden I am to these sorcerer's spells,
Phantasms of my mother's warmth.
The letters form words,
the words weave into wards,
meant to repel
the past and the present,
all the infernos that ascent.

Beholden I am to these pages,
that would put to shame all mages.
Beholden I am to this adventure
that deserves no censure.
Beholden I am to this elixir,
that awakens me, unhinges me, provokes me.
Beholden I am to this gift
that makes me think,
that makes me forget.

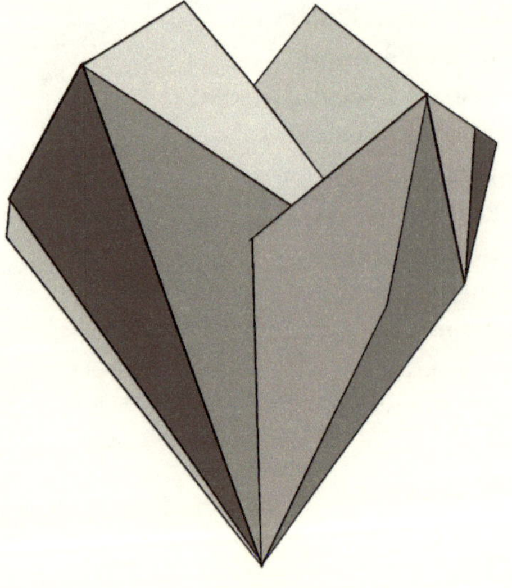

UNFOLD

Unfold, life's too short.
Don't rewind, relive.
Unfold, why waste time?
Breathe, stop, absorb.
Let it go,
like sand through fingers,
like breath that becomes air,
like faith that is laid bare.

Unfold, like a story retold.
Tales are meant to be told
and uncovered in their own time
and rediscovered in time, sometime.

Unfold, lives there aren't a thousand.
Billions have drowned in the sea,
leaving no footprints
on the sands of history.
It's a search for self,
before the self, ceases to be.

Unfold, life's too short
to pretend to be another.
Conning is but a crime;
it is but a waste of time.

Don't slip away, hold on!
Hang on, by the branch
of your own stories,
Not your glories.
Unfold, breathe, repeat.

BURN US

Burn us, leave no traces.
Burn us, like effigies
of those you can't touch.
Burn our voices too,
Why don't you?
But silence us, you can't.

Sati Pratha, birthed by you,
nurtured by you.
Centuries upon centuries
of our ashes;
Cover your conscience.
Bathe us in fire,
but wash away our identities, you can't.

Burn us, leave no traces.
Touch us, choke us.
Blind us to your tyranny
with your poisoned honey.
Cage us, under a pretty glass ceiling,
weave us more bejewelled veils
to hide our very faces,
Hide it from your kind.
Burn us, rape us
but conquer us, you can't.

Impermanence

A loving lover, a melancholy child,
Promises made in the dead of the night,
Footprints have more claim on the sand.
We are and then,
we are no more.
It is a wild rush
for perpetuity.
The children bear the remains,
bound by chains,
to a petty name.
Conquer the transience, the chorus sings.
Fools! Truth can't be conquered,
the ever-expanding evanescence sings back.

THE TINY

Tiny feet beside tiny feet,
not for play, nor for joy.
Tiny hands upon tiny hands,
not for the peals of innocence.

The little turbaned head,
light, like a candy cloud.
The little head, marked with red,
heavy, with a burden unknown.
Both bonded together
by threads of fate,
tied by a sick mind.

The red that burnt away the new bud
is now a sorrowful white.
The painter, the owner of a vulgar mind.
The red shackles,
now broken relics
from a time, the sick mind favoured.

The white is but one of doom,
not one of peace.
The white is but a clarion call for war,
not for that convenient peace.

Our Eternal Love

Twining round and round,
like creepers on a mission,
Tendrils clasped in passion.
Breath mating breath,
strength baiting strength,
futures are made in such fashion.

Drowning in rivers,
that want to meet that sea of completion.
Jigsaw pieces are falling from grace,
falling from grace are these idiotic ways.

We are a team,
you are in our godforsaken seams.
The gods are in love.
Those imbeciles don't know,
the gods thirst for it,
they thirst for our eternal love.

CAMOUFLAGE

Camouflage your emotions,
let it not ruin your disguise.
Bury your pain,
let it not your countrymen misguide.
The shower of rocks is of course, justified.

Do not shoot,
your life is then but moot.
Spill more than you can afford,
expect in return no reward.
Spill blood, not tears,
isn't that what you are paid for?

The canned soup won't help,
You have only yourself to help.
The non-existent jackets will definitely harm,
your mother's prayers will keep you warm.

Your numbers are your only hope,
the archaic weapons from a time of no hope
are but like decorations
in white clothed vultures' palatial houses.

Hold up the flag,
to your broken leg give no slack.

Hold your spirits up too,
or they won't feed your wife and children two.

You will be forgotten
even before you drop dead.
But worry not!
The earth remembers,
the earth remembers and embraces every last bit of you.

THE DIRT

Sweat calls to dirt,
in a cry, centuries old.
Tears turn to blood,
in a play, from a time unknown.

The men on hilltops watch
and then forget
the dirt turning in on itself.
in that rage,
in that race,
for sustenance.

Back against back,
blood against blood.
No space for the dirt to breathe,
no space for the seed to grow,
no space for the mind
to reach towards that mine of gold.

The congested dirt prays
in congested tins
for a breadth of air
there is no space to hope for more.

LITTLE UPSTART

Creeps up your spine,
a creature so well defined.
Its tentacles studded with apprehensions many,
its teeth sharpened with agony.

An intruder with many faces,
it brings to life the dark,
it leaves a tender mark,
in places deep down.

Parasitic creepers,
disappointment reapers,
play hide and seek with your insecurities
and refreshes your injuries.

Break the fourth wall,
roar out the war call,
lash out against that defined formlessness
that seeks in your mind permanence.

Bait it with your tender heart,
trap that little upstart
within your clenched fists.
turn it to mist,
crush it, abuse it,
till it agrees to cease and desist.

THE ABYSS

The abyss beckoned;
to the fall did many succumb.
There is no need to fear
it's just that the second advent is here.

It came riding on the dragon
not by a fraction.
Is subtlety its strong suit.
The wicked, they say, shall soon be moot.

The Kali Yuga-
Three quarters sin,
one quarter virtue.
Oh dear, now that's a lot of wicked
to be pushed to the brim!

Couldn't he use a finer sieve?
Couldn't he forgive
those who are weak,
innocuous and bleak?

This is the Kali Yuga;
we are either feeble or evil
The sieve is pointless;
that which makes it through,
is practically weightless.

Consumed by the abyss
are my scholarship and skills
My heart has bled out too.
Why leave me hanging by the edge?
Come on, take the rest too!

Or better still,
I will take back what's rightfully mine.
We, will take back what's rightfully ours.
For it, remember, we shall strive
till the end of time.

To My Acquaintance ✌

Well acquainted are you
with my thoughts.
So evident are all my blots
How could I construe
that it was all untrue?

You admired only my form;
It has become on my side, a thorn.
You admired the dreamer, the achiever
in your godless way.
To your dismay
I was just a true believer.

Well acquainted were you
with my reservations many
When you begged me to forsake them
was it your intention,
to take advantage of my weak comprehension?

I am no angel;
you are no demon.
You were just being experimental.
It was just, for me, truly baneful.

Now I run from
all that reminds me of that delusional bliss

I now give romantic songs and books
a big miss.

I, now run from all that glistens.
I will from now on
look for iridescence.
Oh, you think I have stopped looking?
Fool, it's just the beginning.

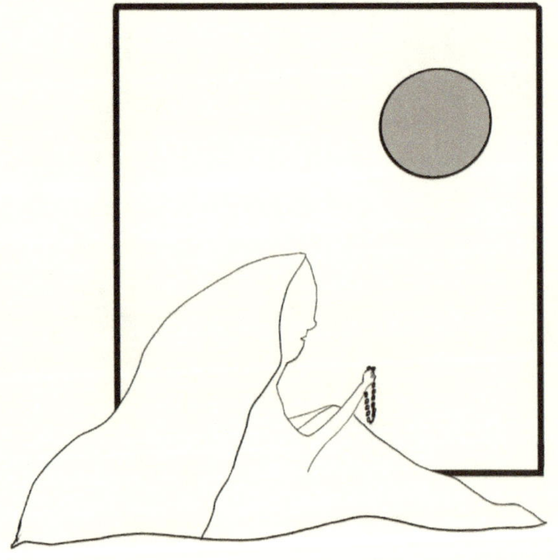

My Angel

The wooden windows
let in the dawn
for the flaxen head,
bend over the hymns,
in praise of the Gods.

The sun wakes up to her prayers
for her troubled progeny
for, there are, you see, many.

On the red soil,
she walks barefoot.
Many a prayers does she chant,
for her cares aren't scant.

The verdant property surrounds her, all sunny;
The birds, the fragrant jasmine, the water apples, the snakes, the
toddy cats,
all give her singular self some company.

Wrapped in a crushed white saree
she is godlier than the gods.
She has left all temptation
for her absent children
who deserve her naught.

He whom she worships
looks at me through her kind eyes
and smiles at me through her toothless smile
and looks over me through her blessings many.
Her touch, gentler than any.

Nature has overtaken her abode.
My Ammoma, my angel
will one day,
get her just award
in the lap of he who rewards.

SHUT UP

Please Shut Up ✺

'Just think, I won't'
Oh dear, please don't.
That advice is worthless
when my mind isn't exactly seamless.

'No need to feel so blue.
Just stop, why don't you?'
An excellent suggestion
just the answer, to every question.

'You are just lazy,
not that crazy,
be rest assured.'
Why, thank you, I am now, reassured.

'Why can't you maintain sobriety?'
Hey, please go ask my anxiety.
He is my best friend,
he won't relent, even on a weekend.

'Just pray,
your life will no longer be grey'
you see, it didn't work out,
to my great dismay.

'It is the Devil's work, a curse.
Oh, things could be worse.
Why don't you cheer up?'
Sure, I will, now please shut up.

www.ingramcontent.com/pod-product-compliance
Lightning Source LLC
LaVergne TN
LVHW041739190726
843493LV00008B/2424